921
CAR

Gleiter, Jan

Kit Carson

DATE DUE

	BRODART	08/90 15.33	

KIT CARSON

Library of Congress Number: 87-4564

Library of Congress Cataloging in Publication Data

Gleiter, Jan, 1947-
    Kit Carson.

    (Raintree stories)
    Summary: a biography of the legendary
American trapper, scout, and Indian agent.
    1. Carson, Kit, 1809-1868—Juvenile
literature.   2. Pioneers—West (U.S.)—
Biography—Juvenile literature.   3. Scouts
and scouting—West (U.S.)—Biography—
Juvenile literature.   4. Soldiers—West (U.S.)
—Biography—Juvenile literature.   5. West
(U.S.)—History—Juvenile literature.
[1. Carson, Kit, 1809-1868. 2. Pioneers.
3. West (U.S.)—Biography] I. Thompson,
Kathleen. II. Whipple, Rick, ill. III. Title.
F592.C33G55   1987   978'.02'0924 [B] [92]   87-4564
ISBN 0-8172-2650-8 (lib. bdg.)
ISBN 0-8172-2654-0 (softcover)

KIT CARSON

Jan Gleiter and Kathleen Thompson

Illustrated by Rick Whipple

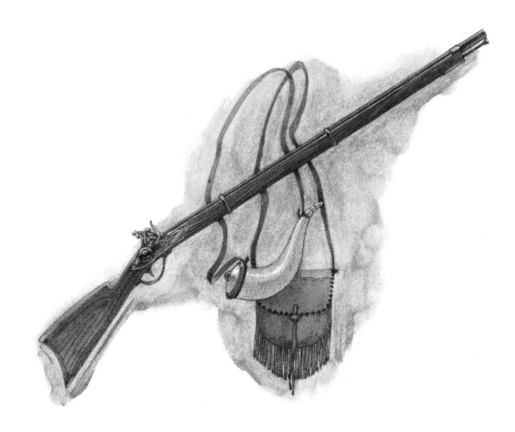

Raintree Childrens Books
Milwaukee

The Carsons and the Boones were never much for settling down. There always seemed to be some new frontier calling to them. That's probably what took them from Scotland to America. And from Pennsylvania to Kentucky. And from Kentucky to Missouri. They always seemed to be happiest when they were exploring some place they'd never seen before. Or finding out about the trails and the forests and the animals in some place where they decided to hang their hats for a while.

In 1811, when young Kit Carson was just two years old, he sat on the back of one of the family's horses on the trip to Missouri. It was a long trip and a hard one. But it took the Carsons to a brand new place.

When Kit was just a few years older, he started hunting and fishing with Daniel Boone. Daniel was an old man by that time, but he remembered everything he'd ever learned about shooting and tracking and the ways of the Indians. And he taught it to young Kit. One of the things Kit learned was to respect the Indians who lived around them.

One day, when Kit was six years old, he was playing by the river near his home. Suddenly, he knew he wasn't alone. In the bushes all around him were small brown faces. Kit waved at the Indian children to join him. Slowly, they came out of the bushes and down to the river.

Kit pointed to himself and said his name. No answer. So Kit pointed again at his own chest and said his name. Then he pointed at one of the other children. The Indian child said his name.

Soon Kit knew all the children's names. Before
long, they had taught him an Indian game that was
played with sticks. Kit showed them a game he
played with his brothers and sisters. They spoke with
different words, but it didn't seem to matter. They
understood each other.

When Kit was fifteen, he went to work as an apprentice for a saddlemaker named Workman. He had to promise to stay for a year. In exchange, Workman would teach him to make saddles. But, as Kit's sister said later, "About the only use he had for a saddle was on a horse's back."

K it wanted the life of the outdoors. He dreamed of the West. He wanted to go buffalo hunting. He wanted to see forts and Spanish missions. He wanted to be a trapper and explore wild and unknown places.

And then one day he heard about a group of traders who were going west, to Santa Fe. Kit's older brothers decided to go with them as far as Independence, Missouri. But they wouldn't let Kit go. He was too young.

Well, Kit thought he was plenty old enough. He had waited a long time, and he was ready. So he borrowed a mule from a neighbor and set out for Independence, a hundred miles away. When he got there, he set the mule loose and hoped it would get back home.

His next job was to talk the traders into taking him along. Kit was not very big, and the traders laughed at him. They said they needed men for the trip, not boys. But Kit didn't give up. One of the leaders decided that this young boy had lots of spirit. He said Kit could come along and take care of the animals.

So Kit started on the long trip to New Mexico.

In November, the caravan of wagons arrived at Santa Fe. With sixty wagons and one hundred men, it was one of the biggest caravans ever to come to that town. Everyone came out to welcome the wagons.

But Kit decided not to stay in Santa Fe. He went with a small group of the traders up to Taos. There he met an old friend of his father's, a trapper and explorer named Kincaid.

All winter Kit stayed with Kincaid in the New Mexico hills. Like Daniel Boone, Kincaid taught Kit all he could. He taught him Spanish and several Indian languages. He taught Kit Indian sign language and the ways of the Southwest Indians.

Kincaid gave Kit geography lessons. They had no books. But Kincaid could draw maps and charts on the ground with a stick, maps of places few people had ever been.

Kit made his own clothes out of furs and animal skins. The two men made beds out of corn husks covered with buffalo robes. Yes, Kit had finally been on a buffalo hunt.

Kit learned how to cook. He also learned how to dry meat so that it would last for a long time without going bad.

And Kit became friends with the Indians who lived in the pueblo near Taos.

When Kit was twenty, a man named Ewing Young came to Santa Fe and Taos looking for men to join a trapping party. He heard about Kit and asked him to go along. It didn't take long for Kit to say yes.

For the next twelve years of his life, Kit trapped and hunted beaver, elk, deer, and buffalo. He joined up with the Rocky Mountain Fur Company. He lived and worked with mountain men like Jim Bridger and Tom Fitzpatrick. But Taos was his home and he always went back there.

Many times, Kit's knowledge of Indian ways got the trappers out of dangerous situations. Kit talked to the Indians he met along the way in their own language or in sign language. Often he was able to keep the trappers and the Indians from fighting. But when there was fighting, Kit fought on the side of the trappers, right or wrong.

On one trip, the trappers set up camp near a group of Arapaho Indians. Kit was twenty-five then. He met a beautiful young Arapaho woman named Waa-nibe. He fell in love with her.

Kit and Waa-nibe were married. Two years later they had a daughter they named Adaline.

Adaline's mother died when she was very young. When Adaline was five, Kit decided to take his daughter back to his family in Missouri. Kit's family welcomed the lively, pretty little girl. She immediately started going to the Rock Springs School.

Kit stayed with his family for a while and then went to St. Louis to do some business. It was on the trip back from St. Louis that Kit met a man who would change his life.

Kit Carson and Lieutenant John Charles Frémont
met on a steamboat. They started talking about
the West. Frémont had just been ordered by the
United States government to explore the country
between Missouri and the Rocky Mountains. He had
been in St. Louis hiring men to go with him. He had
only one problem. The man who was supposed to be
his guide couldn't go.

Kit told Frémont he could take him wherever he
wanted to go. Frémont hired him at once.

Kit Carson guided three exploring trips for
Charles Frémont. Those trips gave Americans
knowledge of huge parts of this continent for the first
time. And they made Kit Carson famous. He became
a legend for his courage and his skills as a guide. He
carried messages from Frémont to officials in
Washington, D.C. And he carried messages back. And
he always got through.

After the last trip with Frémont, Kit went back to Taos. He became the U.S. government's agent to the Ute Indians who had been his friends for so long. Kit Carson had fought Indians most of his life because they were part of the danger of the West. He had also lived with and tried to understand them. Now, he spoke up for them.

Most agents, he said, lied to the Indians. They made empty promises. Many frontier people attacked the Indians and stole their land. Most of the recent Indian wars, he said, were the fault of those agents and frontier people, not the Indians.

Years later, when the oldtimers talked about Kit Carson, they told stories about how he could track anything on two feet or four. They talked about his shooting and his trapping.

But the things most people remembered about Kit were his honesty and his concern for all the people of this country, including the people who were here first.